Callie
A Great Gray Owl

by
Bonnie Highsmith Taylor

Perfection Learning®

Dedication

For Colleen Bulger

About the Author

Bonnie Highsmith Taylor is a native Oregonian. She loves camping in the Oregon mountains and watching birds and other wildlife. Writing is Ms. Taylor's first love. But she also enjoys going to plays and concerts, collecting antique dolls, and listening to good music.

Ms. Taylor is the author of several Animal Adventure books, including *Kip: A Sea Otter* and *Roscoe: A North American Moose.*

Photographs courtesy of Jeff Foott (www.jfoott.com): cover, pp. 5, 7, 8, 9, 10, 12, 14, 16, 20, 23, 24, 25, 28, 29, 30, 31, 33, 35, 36, 37, 38, 39, 40, 42, 44, 45, 47, 49, 50, 52, 53
Photograph courtesy of Windland Rice: p. 43

Some images copyright ArtToday (www.arttoday.com)
Book Design: Randy Messer

Printed in the United States of America. For information, contact Perfection Learning® Corporation, 1000 North Second Avenue, P.O. Box 500, Logan, Iowa 51546-0500.
Tel: 1-800-831-4190 • Fax: 1-712-644-2392

Paperback ISBN 0-7891-5272-x
Cover Craft® ISBN 0-7807-9652-7

In North America, there are 18 species of owls. There are about ⟨130⟩ species in the world.

you know what they had to do...

Callie landed on a limb of a half-dead pine tree. She scanned the area carefully.

There would be good hunting here. There was an open meadow. The owls could hunt mice and voles. They would also find gophers and shrews.

7

But where would she nest? Owls do not usually make their own nests. Some small owls use old woodpecker holes. Larger owls use old nests made by hawks or ravens. Some even nest on the ground.

Callie's mate flew around in a large circle. Suddenly he stopped. He landed on a lodgepole pine tree.

He had found a perfect place. It was probably an old hawk's nest.

He made a low sound. Callie flew to where he perched. She looked the nest over. She rearranged some moss-covered sticks with her beak.

This *was* a good spot. There would be morning sun and afternoon shade.

It would be a good nesting place. It would be a good place for Callie to raise her first family.

The male flew to a nearby limb on a fir tree. Callie flew beside him.

The male put his head close to hers. Callie made low hooting sounds. They preened each other with their beaks. As the preened each other, a strong bond was building. They were growing very close.

One year ago, Callie had hatched out with three other owlets. She was the only female. She had been fed and cared for most of the summer by her parents.

In late summer, she had left her parents and her brothers.

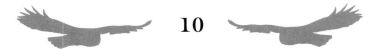

All winter she had cared for herself. It had been a long, hard winter. But she had learned hunting skills from her mother and father.

Great gray owls do not migrate as some birds do. But sometimes they move to a new area when food supplies get low.

Callie had learned to move down low when the snow fell deep. She learned to hunt in fields around farms. There the snow was not so deep.

But even so, the hunting was not always easy. Many times she had gone to sleep hungry.

But now it was spring. There would be good hunting once more. And she had a mate.

Now Callie would raise a family of her own. She would teach them everything she had been taught by her parents. She and her mate would teach their young to be *great gray owls*.

Chapter 2

Callie arranged the nest the way she wanted it. Her mate hunted.

He circled low. He landed on a limb and watched the ground. He must find something. He must prove that he could provide for his mate and the family they would have.

By bringing food to Callie, he would strengthen the bond they had formed.

A small patch of snow moved. It was just below the male owl. It probably was a heather vole.

In the winter, voles live on the ground just under the snow. They make runways in the snow. In the summer, they make nests of dry grass and lichen in burrows underground.

The snow moved once more. In a flash, the male owl swooped down. He grasped the vole in his talons. He bit the back of the vole's head with his beak.

The male ate the head of the vole. He gave Callie the body. The body was the most tender part.

The two owls finished eating. Then they sat side by side and nuzzled.

Callie was a little bigger than her mate. Most female owls are larger than males.

Callie and her mate nibbled the feathers on each other's faces. For several minutes, they preened each other. Callie smoothed her mate's feathers. He rubbed his face against Callie's face. They made soft cooing sounds. Then they sat very still.

Something on the ground drew their attention. They looked down.

A female coyote, heavy with pups, sniffed the ground. She cocked her head to one side. She listened to a movement beneath the snow. She pounced and caught a vole.

The owls watched her swallow it whole. Then the female coyote moved on. She sniffed the ground as she went.

The male owl closed his eyes. Callie closed hers too.

Their toes, or talons, closed tightly
around the limb they were perched on.
Three toes curled around the front of the
limb. The other toe curled around the
back of the limb. They could not fall off
as they slept.

The sun warmed their bodies. It felt
good.

Like all birds, owls have feathers that
insulate them. That means the feathers

keep birds warm in the winter. And they keep birds cool in the summer. By ruffling their feathers, birds keep out the heat or the cold.

After a short nap, the male owl began to hunt again.

Great gray owls hunt in the daytime as well as night. Their ancestors lived mainly in the Far North. At certain times of the year, the days are quite long. The owls did most of their hunting by daylight.

Now great gray owls hunt by day or night. This makes hunting easier for them. They can catch animals that come out in the daytime. And they can catch those that come out at night.

Some owls even catch and eat other owls.

Chapter 3

By the third day, Callie had her nest just the way she wanted it. She had removed two old sticks. And she had added a new one.

Owls do not line their nests with grass or moss as some birds do. They do not use feathers for lining either. They cover their newly hatched babies with feathers. This keeps them warm if the mother owl needs to leave the nest for a short time. The air is still cold when the owlets hatch.

Great gray owls live in thick forests. They sometimes can be found over 4,000 feet high in the mountains. It does not get warm very early in the year. And even when the days are warm, the nights are cold.

Callie and her mate had explored their new area. They knew where the best hunting was.

They found a pond nearby. It would be a good place for taking baths. Owls love to splash in the water.

Their new home was in a remote area. No other owls were using the area.

Owls have territories. And they do not usually go into one anothers' territories. By making a certain sound, owls tell other owls to keep out.

Callie laid her first egg. All that day and night, she sat on it. Her mate brought her a fat vole. She hungrily swallowed it whole.

Her mate flew to a nearby tree. He waited for her to signal if she was still hungry.

While he waited, he closed his eyes. He rested for a while.

Callie dozed also. An hour later, she

made a chirping sound. She wanted food.

Her mate flew to a dead tree near the meadow. He watched the snow-covered ground. He saw no movement. He listened very closely.

Owls have very sharp hearing. The right ear opening is larger and a little higher than the left opening. Each ear has a flap of skin behind and in front of it. The owl can move these flaps. It can move one alone or both together.

An owl can detect sound by turning its head and moving the ear flaps. This helps determine where the sound is coming from.

It is easier to hear an animal moving about when the ground is dry. When there is snow or the ground is wet, the sound is harder to hear.

The male owl could hear a slight sound below.

He watched closely. He looked for movement. Owls' eyes are very sharp. It would be as if you were looking through binoculars.

Penguins and owls are the only birds whose eyes are on the front of their faces. They cannot move their eyes at all. They must turn their heads to make their eyes move. An owl can turn its head nearly all the way around.

The male owl saw a movement in the snow. The snow was not very deep.

Owls can fly without making any sound. That's because they have very soft feathers on their wings.

Silently, the male owl swooped down. He grasped a vole in his sharp talons. In a split second, he bit off its head and swallowed it.

Then he took the rest to his mate. Callie gulped it down. Now she was full.

It would be a while before she was hungry again. Then she would signal her mate. And he would bring her a juicy vole or a mouse.

The male would feed his mate for about six weeks. He would feed her for the four weeks she sat on the eggs. And he would feed her until the chicks were about two weeks old.

After that, the owls would share the feeding of the chicks. They would do that until the chicks could take care of themselves.

Chapter 4

*D*uring the next week, Callie laid two more eggs.

Every day, it grew warmer. At last, all the snow melted away.

Callie got tired sitting on the nest day and night.

Sometimes she would hop to the limb just below the nest. She would stretch. She would flap her wings. She would preen her feathers.

But she couldn't stay off the eggs for very long. If they got chilled, they would not hatch.

One day, it was very warm. Callie had been sitting on her eggs for about three weeks. She was uncomfortable.

Her mate landed on a nearby tree. He was dripping wet. He had bathed in the pond not far from the nest.

He shook himself hard. Then he started preening his feathers.

Callie thought how cool a quick dip in the pond would be. She flew from the nest to the pond. Her mate followed her. While she splashed in the water, he sat on a log. He continued to preen himself. He ruffled his feathers.

All at once, Callie saw something. An animal was climbing the tree where her nest was. She flew

from the pond. Her feathers were wet and heavy.

She landed on the animal. It was a pine marten. Her talons went deep into its neck. The marten snarled. It bared its teeth.

Callie pulled her claws out. The marten fell to the ground. It landed with a thud. For a moment, it lay still. Then it got to its feet and staggered into the woods.

Pine martens are weasel-like animals. They are only one of the many animals that rob nests. Raccoons, possums, and even bobcats steal eggs and baby birds from nests.

Large birds, like hawks and eagles, eat other birds' eggs and chicks.

Sometimes eggs and small chicks are blown from nests in bad storms.

Callie shook herself dry. She returned to her nest. Her eggs were safe. And she had taken a nice bath.

Chapter 5

The first owlet to hatch was a female. She used a little, white "egg tooth" on the tip of her beak to break the shell. She was almost naked. Her skin was pink. And her eyes were tightly closed.

She made soft peeping sounds. Callie looked her baby over. Then Callie tucked the owlet back under her body with the other two eggs. They were not ready to hatch.

All day, Callie sat on the new chick and the eggs. The male owl brought her food. He caught some voles and a gopher. He ate most of the gopher himself.

It took a lot of time to feed even one chick. Callie had to tear the meat into small pieces.

The owlet had a hard time swallowing. She gulped at the chunks of vole. They kept falling out of her mouth. Callie would push them back in.

Her mate perched on a nearby tree and watched.

When the owlet was full, it slept. Callie sat still and rested. The sun sank low. The air grew cool. Callie fluffed her feathers. She had to keep her chick warm.

Below, two does walked out of the trees. They stopped in the meadow. Callie watched them as they grazed. The new grass shoots were tender and sweet.

The next day, another chick hatched. It was a male. Two days later, the third one hatched. It was another female.

Callie's mate was kept very busy feeding his family. After the chicks and his mate were fed, he would feed himself.

Owls do not digest all of their food. They do not digest bones, teeth, hair, feathers, or claws. Owls swallow most of their food whole.

After a few hours, the parts that do not digest form a lump. The lump is called a *pellet*. The bones, claws, and teeth of the owl's prey are packed tightly in the pellet. The hair and feathers wrap around the outside of the pellet.

The owl coughs out the pellet. Large owls cough out large pellets. Small owls cough out small pellets. Even owls who eat only insects cough out pellets. They do not digest the hard shells of beetles.

Most owls have no trouble coughing out their pellets. They are coated with slime. This makes them pop out easily.

But a few owls have trouble. They have to open and shut their beaks and shake their heads hard to make the pellets pop out. Sometimes it takes as long as ten minutes.

Most of the time owls spit out their pellets in the same place. Pellets are usually under a tree limb where owls roost or beneath a nest.

People who study owls collect their pellets. Then they can tell what kind of prey the owl has eaten.

At the end of two weeks, the chicks were covered with soft, downy feathers. Their eyes were open. The pupils of their eyes had a cloudy look. When they were about two months old, the pupils turned black.

An owl's big, round eyes give it a look of wisdom. When someone is very intelligent, he is said to be "wise as an owl."

Scientists believe that geese, ravens, and crows are smarter than owls. But an owl is the best hunter of all birds.

Chapter 6

*M*any songbirds had returned to the forest. Bluebirds were hunting for nest holes in dead trees.

Grosbeaks were gathering nesting material. They would make their nests high in the air at the ends of tree branches.

Swallows were flying about. They were trying to beat the bluebirds to the holes in the trees.

The three owlets watched the other birds flying about. They wanted to fly too. But they were not quite ready. They still had to lose their fluffy down. Then they would grow flight feathers.

The owlets flapped their wings. They flopped around in the nest. This was the way they exercised.

Callie left the young owls in the nest alone more often now. But she did not go far away.

There were many dangers in the forest. Raccoons and martens could climb the tree and eat the owls. The owlets could fall from the nest and be killed. Or they could be caught by coyotes or other animals.

Early one morning, the owlets watched a porcupine waddle out of an opening in a pile of rocks. Following behind was a baby porcupine. The baby had been born the day before.

As the owlets watched, the porcupines went toward the pond. The mother porcupine would feast on the skunk cabbage that was blooming there.

The firstborn owlet leaned out of the nest to watch. Suddenly, she fell! Down, down, down she went. She cried loudly.

Callie was not far away. She flew to her chick. She was frantic. Around and around the chick she went.

Callie's wild screeches rang out. Her mate soared across the meadow and landed beside her. Above, the other two wide-eyed owlets watched.

The fallen chick flopped around on the ground. For a long time, she flapped her wings. She cheeped and cheeped.

After a while, she lay still. The male owl flew to a tree. But Callie stayed beside her chick.

The chick's heart pounded. She was so tired. She finally fell asleep.

Callie stayed close. She made low clucking sounds.

After nearly an hour, the chick woke up. She got to her feet. She looked up at the nest.

Suddenly, she jumped onto the trunk of the tree. She began to climb. The chick fell back to the ground.

Again, she jumped onto the trunk of the tree. She climbed. Her sharp little talons sank into the bark. She used her beak to pull herself up.

Several times, she stopped to rest, hanging on tightly.

Callie flew around and around the tree. She cooed softly.

After a long time, the owlet reached the nest. She lay still and panted.

Callie flew to the nest. She nuzzled the chick. She nuzzled the other two chicks.

The male owl flew away to hunt for food. He returned with a fat gopher. The owl family ate their fill. Then the little ones slept.

By the time the owlets were about six weeks old, they had their flight feathers. They could fly a little but not enough to be on their own. All the chicks had left the nest. They roosted on tree limbs with their mother and father.

Callie fed them on the ground. They did not need their food torn in small pieces anymore.

One day, Callie flew to where her three chicks were on the ground. She had a mouse in her beak.

The owlets opened their mouths wide. But Callie held on to the mouse. She flew to a tree limb. It was about 20 feet away.

The chicks looked up at her. They made hissing sounds. They ran around in circles, looking at their mother. But Callie remained on the limb. She held the mouse in her beak.

At last, the oldest chick flew to the limb. She took the mouse from Callie.

Every day, Callie made the chicks fly to a limb to be fed. She moved farther away each time. By late summer, the young owls had learned to hunt.

The adult owls were molting. They were losing their old feathers. When winter came, they would have all new feathers.

By fall, the young birds were able to take care of themselves. Two of them left the area. They would find their own territories. One chick stayed with its parents. She was the one that had been born last. In the spring, she would leave too. The adult owls probably would never see their young ones again.

But next spring, Callie and her mate would raise a new family. Probably in the same nest where their first three chicks had been born.

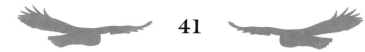

There are many species of owls in North America. The smallest are elf owls. They are about the size of a sparrow. They are not much more than six inches long.

Elf owls live mostly in deserts in the Southwest. They nest in old woodpecker holes, trees, or large cactus plants. The inside of a cactus never

Elf owl

gets too hot or too cold. It is a good place to hatch eggs.

Elf owls eat grasshoppers, moths, beetles, caterpillars, crickets, and spiders. They can catch insects in midair with their talons.

Next in size are ferruginous and pygmy owls. They look a lot alike. They are about seven inches long.

Ferruginous owls live in Arizona, New Mexico, and western Texas. They don't usually hunt in the daytime. They hunt early in the morning and evening. These owls are sometimes mistaken for bats.

Pygmy owls live in the high mountains of the western United States. They also live in parts of Canada.

Pygmy owl

Even though quite small, they are very fierce. They will attack animals much bigger than themselves. Besides insects, pygmy owls eat reptiles, birds, and many small mammals.

In some ways, pygmy owls are different from most owls. Most owls can fly without making a sound. The wings of pygmy owls make a whirring sound when they fly. Another difference is that pygmy owls take the fur and feathers off their prey before they eat it.

Flammulated owl

Flammulated owls also live in the forests of the western United States and Canada. They eat mice and other small animals. They are the only small North American owls that have dark brown eyes. Most owls have yellow eyes.

Saw-whet owl

Saw-whet owls make sounds like saws being sharpened. *Whet* means "to sharpen by rubbing with a stone."

These little birds are quite tame. A person can walk up to them while they are resting.

They live in forests and nest in old woodpecker holes. The chicks are a dark chocolate brown. As they grow older, they look more like their parents. They are light brown, speckled with white.

Saw-whet owls are night hunters. They

feed on insects and small mammals, including bats. They also catch and eat birds.

Boreal owls are another very tame bird. People who band wild birds can catch them in their hands.

They are a lot like the saw-whet owls. They look almost the same. They nest in tree hollows.

Boreal owls live mostly in the Far North. They can be found from Alaska east to Newfoundland. *Boreal* means "northern."

Burrowing owls are about nine to eleven inches long. Their legs are longer than most owls' legs. When someone walks toward them, they will bow and bob up and down.

Burrowing owl

 **45**

They are active in the daytime. They live in deserts and plains where prairie dogs and ground squirrels live.

Burrowing owls nest in colonies in deserted burrows. But they often dig burrows of their own. They have been seen nesting in burrows on golf courses and airport fields.

Their nesting chambers can be up to 20 feet long. They lay more eggs than most owls—from six to eleven. Unlike most owls, they line their nests with grass and weeds. They've even been known to use pieces of cow manure.

They are different from most owls in other ways too. Besides small rodents, lizards, and snakes, they eat the fruit of the prickly pear cactus. And they can make a sound like a rattlesnake. Even the chicks can make this sound. It scares intruders away from their nest.

Males sit on the eggs the same as females do. This is not true of other owls.

Another thing they do is store food. In one burrow, more than 75 dead mice were found by people who study owls. The burrowing owls who nest together share this food in the winter. Other owls do not group together.

Long-eared owls and great horned owls look a lot alike. Long-eared owls have two bunches of feathers on their heads that look like ears. They are ear tufts. The great horned owls' *ear tufts* are called *horns*.

Great horned owls are larger. They can grow up to 24 inches long. Long-eared owls are only about 15 inches long.

Great horned owl

 **47**

Great horned owls are common in all of North America. They make their nests in old hawks' nests or on cliffs. They add feathers from their breasts to their nests. They lay two or three eggs.

Great horned owls feed on many animals. They eat rabbits, rodents, crows, ducks, and other birds. They even eat other owls. They will kill and eat skunks. And they can even kill porcupines. They can swallow an animal one-third their own size.

Unfortunately, great horned owls often carry off domestic animals. These include chickens and other fowl, cats, and small dogs or puppies.

Because of this, there are some areas where the owls are not protected. All other owls are protected by law.

Long-eared owls feed mostly on rodents and insects. Sometimes they add

leaves and chunks of bark to their nests. They use nests that other large birds have left.

Short-eared owls grow to about 17 inches long. They live in meadows and marshes. They nest on the ground in tall grass or weeds.

Short-eared owl chick

Short-eared owls feed mostly on field mice and other small rodents. But if food is scarce, they will eat songbirds. They hunt mainly at dawn and dusk.

If they are cornered while nesting, they hump their backs and spread their wings. They try to look much bigger than they are. They will snap their beaks again and again at an intruder.

Screech owls are found in nearly all parts of the United States. They can be seen in woods, orchards, and backyards.

They nest in tree cavities and nesting boxes made by people. They may use the same nesting site year after year.

Screech owls lay and hatch one egg at a time. If food is scarce, they may only hatch one or two chicks in a year. If there is plenty of food, they may hatch as many as five chicks.

Screech owl

Screech owls are about nine or ten inches long. They eat mice, insects, reptiles, and frogs.

Whiskered owls are almost identical to screech owls. They are called "whiskered" because of the brown and white feathers that grow out of their cheeks. These feathers are stiff like whiskers.

They usually nest in holes in white oak trees. They are quite common in canyons in Arizona. There are also some in New Mexico. They live in very remote areas of forests between 4,000 and 7,000 feet high. Very few people have ever seen whiskered owls.

Hawk owls have small heads and long tails. They fly like hawks. They can fly faster than most owls.

Hawk owl

They live in the forests of the Far North. Hawk owls have become day feeders. They eat a lot of lemmings. Lemmings are active day and night. In the winter when lemmings stay in runways under the snow, hawk owls feed on grouse and other birds.

Hawk owls nest in woodpecker holes or in the hollow ends of broken-off, dead trees. They lay three to nine eggs.

These owls do something quite clever. When they see a game bird shot by a hunter, they carry it off before the hunter can get to it.

Spotted owls and barred owls are the only large owls with dark eyes.

Barred owls are often called "hoot owls." They make very strange sounds. It sounds like they are asking, "Who cooks for you? Who cooks for you all?" One of their calls sounds like people laughing.

Barred owl

They usually hunt at night. They eat rabbits and other small mammals. Their favorite foods are frogs and fish.

Barred owls lay two to four eggs in old hawks' nests or in tree cavities.

Spotted owls are the most endangered owl of all. For many years they have lived

in the old-growth forests of the Pacific Northwest. But due to heavy, clear-cut logging, their habitat has been reduced by 90 percent. Recovery plans for the

Spotted owl

spotted owl include logging bans.

Spotted owls live on mice, rabbits, and squirrels. They nest in caves, tree cavities, and old nests. They raise two to four chicks a year.

No owls are more beautiful than large snowy owls. Their white bodies are covered with gray-brown spots. Snowy

Snowy owl

owls live in the Far North. They feed on lemmings, snowshoe hares, fish, rodents, and waterfowl. They also eat *carrion,* or dead animals.

 **53**

Snowy owls lay up to ten eggs in nests on the ground. Foxes often eat some of the chicks. During the breeding season, snowy owls make noises like barking. But in the winter, they are usually silent.

Barn owls look different from other owls. This is because they are in a different family. There are ten species of barn owls. All the other owls are in the typical owl family.

Barn owl

Barn owls' faces are heart-shaped instead of round like other owls.

These owls are helpful to people. One barn owl eats about 2,000 rats and mice in one year. A pair of barn owls can catch more mice and rats than a dozen cats.

They nest in barns and other buildings. They also take over old

woodchuck and badger dens. They raise about six or seven chicks a year.

Barn owls live in most parts of the United States. But they are not usually found in the Far North.

For more information, contact
The Raptor Center
1920 Fitch Ave.
St. Paul, MN 55108
www.raptor.cvm.umn.edu
email: raptor@umn.edu
phone: (612) 624-4745
fax: (612) 624-8740